Simple & Delicious

FAST FOOD

Simple & Delicious

FAST FOOD

OVER 100 SENSATIONAL RECIPES FOR FAST FOOD LOVERS

This edition published in 2013
LOVE FOOD is an imprint of Parragon Books Ltd

Parragon
Chartist House
15–17 Trim Street
Bath, BA1 1HA, UK

ISBN: 978-1-78186-775-4

Printed in China

Cover design by Geoff Borin
Additional photography by Clive Streeter
Additional home economy by Angela Drake
Introduction by Anne Sheasby

Notes for the Reader
This book uses both metric and imperial measurements. Follow the same units of measurement throughout; do not mix metric and imperial. All spoon measurements are level: teaspoons are assumed to be 5 ml, and tablespoons are assumed to be 15 ml. Unless otherwise stated, milk is assumed to be full fat, eggs and individual vegetables are medium, and pepper is freshly ground black pepper. Unless otherwise stated, all root vegetables should be washed in plain water and peeled prior to using.

For best results, use a food thermometer when cooking meat and poultry – check the latest government guidelines for current advice.

Garnishes, decorations and serving suggestions are all optional and not necessarily included in the recipe ingredients or method.

The times given are an approximate guide only. Preparation times differ according to the techniques used by different people and the cooking times may also vary from those given. Optional ingredients, variations or serving suggestions have not been included in the time calculations.

Recipes using raw or very lightly cooked eggs should be avoided by infants, the elderly, pregnant women, convalescents and anyone suffering from an illness. Pregnant and breastfeeding women are advised to avoid eating peanuts and peanut products. Sufferers from nut allergies should be aware that some of the ready-made ingredients used in the recipes in this book may contain nuts. Always check the packaging before use.

Vegetarians should be aware that some of the ready-made ingredients used in the recipes in this book may contain animal products. Always check the packaging before use.

Contents

Introduction

Fast food does not always mean ready-meals, takeaways, burgers or pizza deliveries. It can just as easily mean delicious home-cooked food that is quick and easy to prepare. Home-cooked fast food delivers fabulous flavour and is perfect for family suppers or snacks. This cookbook features fresh fast food at its very best – simple, speedy, delicious and nutritious.

Speedy Suppers in 30 Minutes or Less

Quick and simple cooking methods conveniently lend themselves to fast cooking. Cooking techniques such as stir-frying, sautéing, steaming, pan-frying, grilling, griddling or microwaving are ideal for creating flavourful fast food. Roasting is good for cooking small cuts of meat, poultry or fish, and is also suitable for small chunks of vegetables or baby vegetables.

Fast & Fresh Ingredients

Fresh, flavourful ingredients play an important role in home-cooked fast food and it is both practical and economical to make the most of foods in season, especially fruits and vegetables. Check out your local farm shops or farmers' markets to see what they can provide, and make the most of fresh foods on offer in the supermarket.

If you have a freezer, buy extra seasonal fruit and vegetables and freeze favourites for use later in the year. Frozen fruits such as mixed berries or summer fruits are ideal for many quick and delicious desserts.

If you have some spare time, perhaps one weekend, cook up a batch of soups, casseroles, chillies, curries, pizzas or pies and freeze in handy individual or family-sized portions, then simply defrost and reheat for a satisfying mid-week meal. It is essential to have a sufficiently stocked store cupboard, so that if you are in a hurry, you can rustle up a tasty supper at short notice with the help of a few kitchen cupboard staples.

Flavour Boosters

Fresh herbs are ideal for fast food, but some dried herbs and many spices add important flavour to dishes. Bouillon powder or stock cubes are a good way to add quick flavour to stocks, soups and sauces. Bottled sauces such as soy sauce, chilli sauce, Tabasco, Worcestershire sauce and tomato ketchup will add a flavour boost to many dishes. Jars of pesto, sun-dried tomatoes, roasted peppers, artichokes, olives, olive pastes, mustards, capers, etc., are good for adding extra taste to sauces, dressings, pizzas, pasta dishes, and so on.

Canned Beans & Vegetables

Canned beans and pulses are essential for fast food and add bulk, texture and flavour. Canned vegetables, especially canned tomatoes, add good flavour to a wide range of recipes. Some dried vegetables such as mushrooms, once rehydrated, add extra taste to sauces, soups, risottos, etc.

Pasta, Rice & Other Grains

Dried pasta, rice and other grains such as couscous, bulgur wheat, quinoa and polenta are essential for many fast and tasty dishes. Pasta, fresh or dried, is quick to cook and very versatile. Served simply with a tasty homemade sauce, pasta creates a filling and flavourful supper. Noodles also make an ideal quick-cooking accompaniment for stir-fries and warm salads, and rice is perfect for risottos, pilaffs and rice salads.

Oils & Vinegars

Keep two or three bottles of oil in your store cupboard – perhaps a light olive or sunflower oil for cooking and a fruity extra virgin olive oil for salad dressings, pesto sauces, etc. Sesame oil is great for stir-fries, and fragrant nut oils such as hazelnut or walnut oil are perfect for extra-special dressings.

Vinegars add flavour to dressings, sauces and stews, so keep a small selection such as cider vinegar, white and/or red wine vinegar and good-quality balsamic vinegar.

Desserts in a Dash

Ready-to-eat dried fruits create a wonderful basis for fruit salads and compotes, and canned fruits are good for simple fruit salads. Fresh fruit requires little preparation but if grilled, roasted or lightly cooked it also provides a simple and delicious dessert.

Have a selection of nuts to hand to add flavour and crunch to salads, rice dishes, stuffings, coatings, crumble toppings and so on.

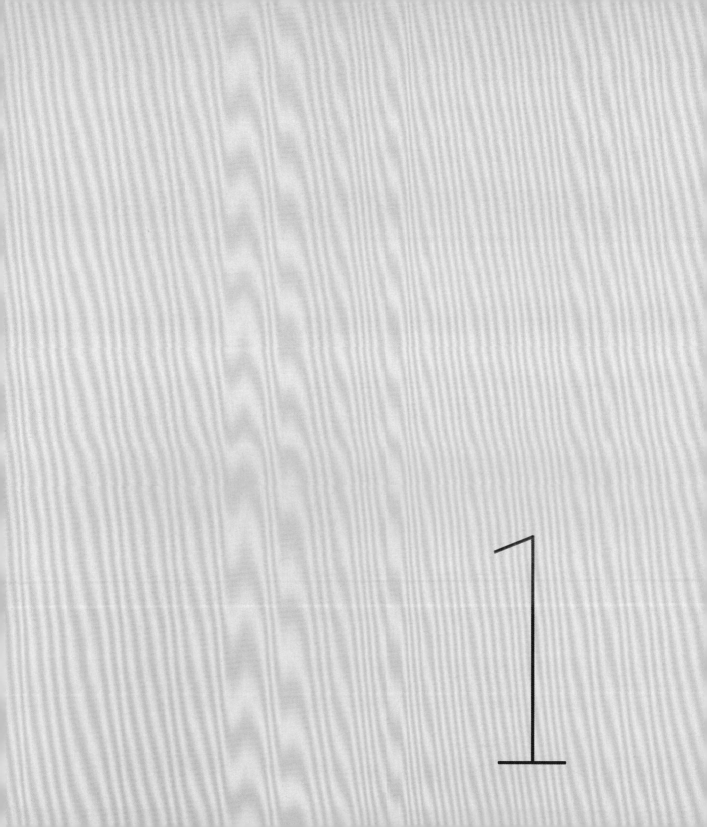

Meat &
Poultry

Griddled Steak with Tomatoes & Garlic

serves 4

3 tbsp olive oil, plus extra for brushing

700 g/1 lb 9 oz tomatoes, peeled and chopped

1 red pepper, deseeded and chopped

1 onion, chopped

2 garlic cloves, finely chopped

1 tbsp chopped fresh flat-leaf parsley

1 tsp dried oregano

1 tsp sugar

4 entrecôte or rump steaks, about 175 g/6 oz each

salt and pepper

freshly cooked new potatoes and French beans, to serve

Put the oil, tomatoes, red pepper, onion, garlic, parsley, oregano and sugar in a heavy-based saucepan and season to taste with salt and pepper. Bring to the boil, then reduce the heat and simmer, uncovered, for 15 minutes.

Meanwhile, preheat a griddle pan over a high heat. Snip any fat around the outsides of the steaks. Season each generously with pepper (no salt) and brush with oil. When the griddle pan is very hot, add the steaks and cook for 1 minute on each side. Reduce the heat to medium and cook according to taste; 1½–2 minutes on each side for rare; 2½–3 minutes on each side for medium; or 3–4 minutes on each side for well done.

Transfer the steaks to warmed individual plates and spoon the sauce over. Serve immediately, accompanied by freshly cooked new potatoes and French beans.

Griddled Steak with Hot Chilli Salsa

serves 4

4 sirloin steaks,
about 225 g/8 oz each

sunflower oil, for brushing

salt and pepper

for the hot chilli salsa

4 fresh red habanero or
Scotch bonnet chillies

4 fresh green poblano
chillies

3 tomatoes, peeled,
deseeded and diced

2 tbsp chopped fresh
coriander

1 tbsp red wine vinegar

2 tbsp olive oil

salt

a few leaves of lamb's
lettuce, to garnish

To make the salsa, preheat the grill to high. Arrange the chillies on a baking sheet and cook under the preheated grill, turning frequently, until blackened and charred. Leave to cool. When cool enough to handle, peel off the skins. Halve and deseed the chillies, then finely chop the flesh.

Mix the chillies, tomatoes and coriander together in a bowl. Whisk the vinegar and oil together in a jug, season to taste with salt and pour over the salsa. Toss well, cover and chill in the refrigerator until required.

Heat a ridged, cast-iron griddle pan over a medium heat and brush lightly with oil. Season the steaks to taste with salt and pepper, add to the griddle pan and cook for 2–4 minutes on each side, or until cooked to your liking. Serve immediately with the salsa, garnished with a few leaves of lamb's lettuce.

Steak in Orange Sauce

serves 4

2 large oranges

25 g/1 oz butter

4 fillet steaks, about 175 g/6 oz each, at room temperature

6 tbsp beef stock

1 tbsp balsamic vinegar

salt and pepper

fresh flat-leaf parsley leaves, to garnish

freshly cooked sugarsnap peas, to serve

Using a zester, pare a few strips of orange zest from 1 orange and reserve for the garnish. Cut the oranges in half, then cut off 4 thin slices and reserve for the garnish. Squeeze the juice from the remaining halves and set aside. Melt the butter in a heavy-based frying pan over a medium heat.

Add the steaks and cook for 1–2 minutes on each side, or until browned and sealed. Transfer the steaks to a warmed plate, season to taste with salt and pepper and set aside, covering with foil to keep warm.

Pour the orange juice into the frying pan and add the stock and balsamic vinegar. Simmer over a low heat for 2 minutes. Season the orange sauce to taste with salt and pepper and return the steaks to the frying pan. Heat through gently for 2 minutes, or according to taste. Transfer to warmed serving plates and garnish with the orange slices, orange zest and parsley leaves. Serve immediately, accompanied by freshly cooked sugarsnap peas.

Beef & Blue Cheese Wraps

serves 4

250 g/9 oz sirloin steak

1 tbsp olive oil

1 tbsp mayonnaise

125 g/4½ oz Stilton cheese, crumbled

4 x 25-cm/10-inch wraps

½ small bag watercress

salt and pepper

Season the steak with salt and pepper.

Preheat a non-stick pan until almost smoking. Add the oil, then seal the steak, cooking on both sides for 30 seconds. Remove from the pan and set aside for a few minutes. Once the steak has rested, cut into thin strips with a sharp knife.

Mix together the mayonnaise and Stilton cheese.

Preheat a non-stick pan or griddle pan until almost smoking, then cook the wraps one at a time on both sides for 10 seconds. This will add some colour and also soften the wraps.

Divide the steak between the wraps, placing it along the middle of each wrap. Top with the Stilton and mayonnaise, and then with watercress, reserving a little for garnish. Roll up, cut in half and serve, garnished with the remaining watercress.

Roast Beef & Coleslaw

serves 1

1 tbsp finely chopped fresh ginger or horseradish sauce

20 g/¾ oz butter, softened

2 slices light rye bread, preferably with caraway

½ small white cabbage, thinly sliced

1 small carrot, coarsely grated

1 spring onion, sliced

1 large slice roast beef

salt and pepper

dill pickles, to serve (optional)

Preheat the grill to a medium–high setting. Mix the ginger with the butter.

Spread one slice of bread generously with some of the ginger butter. Top with the cabbage, trimming any overhanging shreds and placing them back on the middle of the sandwich. Top with grated carrot and spring onion, keeping them away from the edge. Season lightly.

Spread a little of the ginger butter on one side of the beef and lay it, butter down, on the carrot. Spread the remaining butter on the second slice of bread and place it on top of the sandwich, buttered side down.

Put the sandwich on the rack in the grill pan and toast on both sides until crisp and golden. Serve at once with dill pickles, if using.

Spicy Beef & Noodle Soup

serves 4

1 litre/1¾ pints beef stock

150 ml/5 fl oz vegetable or groundnut oil

85 g/3 oz dried rice vermicelli noodles

2 shallots, thinly sliced

2 garlic cloves, crushed

2.5-cm/1-inch piece fresh ginger, thinly sliced

225 g/8 oz fillet steak, cut into thin strips

2 tbsp Thai green curry paste

2 tbsp Thai soy sauce

1 tbsp Thai fish sauce

chopped fresh coriander, to garnish

Pour the stock into a large saucepan and bring to the boil. Meanwhile, heat the oil in a preheated wok or large frying pan. Add about one third of the noodles and cook, stirring, for 10–20 seconds until puffed up. Lift out with tongs, drain on kitchen paper and set aside. Pour off all but 2 tablespoons of the oil from the wok.

Add the shallots, garlic and ginger to the wok and stir-fry for 1 minute. Add the beef and curry paste and stir-fry for 3–4 minutes until tender.

Transfer the beef mixture to the saucepan of stock with the uncooked noodles, soy sauce and fish sauce. Simmer for 2–3 minutes until the noodles have swelled. Serve hot, garnished with chopped coriander and the reserved crispy noodles.

Pork with Mixed Green Beans

serves 4

2 tbsp vegetable or groundnut oil

2 shallots, chopped

225 g/8 oz pork fillet, thinly sliced

2.5-cm/1-inch piece fresh galangal or ginger, thinly sliced

2 garlic cloves, chopped

300 ml/10 fl oz chicken stock

4 tbsp chilli sauce

4 tbsp crunchy peanut butter

115 g/4 oz fine French beans

115 g/4 oz frozen broad beans

115 g/4 oz runner beans, sliced

crispy noodles, to serve

Heat the oil in a preheated wok or large frying pan over a high heat. Add the shallots, pork, galangal and garlic and stir-fry for 3–4 minutes until the pork is lightly browned all over.

Add the stock, chilli sauce and peanut butter and cook, stirring, until the peanut butter has melted. Add all the beans, stir well and simmer for 3–4 minutes, or until tender and the pork is cooked through. Serve immediately with crispy noodles.

Red Curry Pork with Peppers

serves 4–6

2 tbsp vegetable or groundnut oil

1 onion, roughly chopped

2 garlic cloves, chopped

450 g/1 lb pork fillet, thickly sliced

1 red pepper, deseeded and cut into squares

175 g/6 oz mushrooms, quartered

2 tbsp red Thai curry paste

115 g/4 oz creamed coconut, chopped

300 ml/10 fl oz hot pork or vegetable stock

2 tbsp Thai soy sauce

4 tomatoes, peeled, deseeded and chopped

handful of fresh coriander, chopped

Heat the oil in a preheated wok or large frying pan over a medium–high heat. Add the onion and garlic and stir-fry for 1–2 minutes, or until soft but not brown.

Add the pork slices and stir-fry for 2–3 minutes until browned all over. Add the red pepper, mushrooms and curry paste.

Meanwhile, dissolve the coconut in a bowl of hot stock. Add to the pan with the soy sauce. Bring to the boil, then reduce the heat and simmer for 4–5 minutes until the liquid has reduced and thickened.

Add the tomatoes and coriander and cook, stirring, for 1–2 minutes before serving.

Spaghetti alla Carbonara

serves 4

450 g/1 lb dried spaghetti

1 tbsp olive oil

225 g/8 oz rindless pancetta or streaky bacon, chopped

4 eggs

5 tbsp single cream

2 tbsp freshly grated Parmesan cheese

salt and pepper

Bring a large, heavy-based saucepan of lightly salted water to the boil. Add the pasta, return to the boil and cook for 8–10 minutes, or until tender but still firm to the bite.

Meanwhile, heat the oil in a heavy-based frying pan. Add the pancetta and cook over a medium heat, stirring frequently, for 8–10 minutes.

Beat the eggs with the cream in a small bowl and season to taste with salt and pepper. Drain the pasta and return it to the saucepan. Tip in the contents of the frying pan, then add the egg mixture and half the Parmesan cheese. Stir well, then transfer to a warmed serving dish. Serve immediately, sprinkled with the remaining cheese.

Ham & Cheese Croissant

serves 1

1 croissant

2 thin slices cooked ham, halved

mustard (optional)

2 slices hard cheese, such as Cheddar, Gruyère or Emmenthal (about 25 g/1 oz)

1 egg, hard-boiled and sliced (optional)

Preheat the grill to a medium–high setting. Slice the croissant horizontally in half, then lay it, cut sides up, on the rack in the grill pan.

Top each croissant half with a slice of cooked ham, overlapping the halves, and spread with a little mustard, if liked. Then top with the cheese, cutting and overlapping the cheese slices to fit the croissant. Grill for about 2 minutes, until the cheese has melted. The croissant will be warmed through and beginning to brown around the edges.

If including the egg, overlap the slices on the bottom layer. Use a knife to scoop any melted cheese off the foil and on to the croissant, then invert the top in place. Serve at once.

Salami, Pepper & Pine Nut Panini

serves 2

1 large red pepper, deseeded and cut into thin strips

2 garlic cloves, sliced

olive oil

2 panini rolls or individual ciabatta, split horizontally

6 salami slices

handful of fresh basil leaves

1 tbsp pine nuts

1 small head radicchio or chicory

Parmesan or pecorino shavings

Preheat the grill to a medium–high setting. Lay a piece of cooking foil on the rack in the grill pan. Mix the pepper strips and garlic in a heap on the foil. Drizzle with a little olive oil, turn the strips to coat them lightly and then spread them out.

Lay the bread halves cut sides down on the foil around the pepper strips. Cook for about 1 minute to lightly toast the breads, then remove them and continue cooking the pepper strips for 2–3 minutes or until they begin to brown.

Replace the breads on the foil, cut sides up. Cover the bottom layers of bread with the salami and basil leaves. Add the pepper strips and sprinkle with the pine nuts. Cut the radicchio into wedges and arrange them on top. Drizzle with a little oil and grill for 2–3 minutes, until beginning to wilt and brown at the edges. Remove the top layers of bread as soon as they are toasted.

Sprinkle with Parmesan, add the bread tops and serve immediately.

Catalan Toasts

serves 8

2 garlic cloves

2 large tomatoes

8 slices day-old French bread or small rounds country bread or sourdough bread, about 2-cm/¾-inch thick

choice of toppings such as slices of serrano ham, slices of Manchego cheese or pieces of roasted red pepper (optional)

3 tbsp Spanish extra virgin olive oil

pepper

Preheat the grill to high. Halve the garlic cloves. Coarsely grate the tomatoes into a bowl, discarding the skins left in your hand, and season to taste with pepper.

Toast the bread slices under the grill until lightly golden brown on both sides. While the bread slices are still warm, rub with the cut side of the garlic halves to flavour, then top with the grated tomatoes. If using, add a slice of ham or Manchego cheese or a piece of roasted red pepper. Drizzle each with a little of the oil and serve immediately.

Pepperoni Pasta

serves 4

3 tbsp olive oil

1 onion, chopped

1 red pepper, deseeded and diced

1 orange pepper, deseeded and diced

800 g/1 lb 12 oz canned chopped tomatoes in juice

1 tbsp sun-dried tomato paste

1 tsp paprika

225 g/8 oz pepperoni sausage, sliced

2 tbsp chopped fresh flat-leaf parsley, plus extra to garnish

450 g/1 lb dried penne

salt and pepper

Heat 2 tablespoons of the oil in a large, heavy-based frying pan over a medium heat. Add the onion and cook, stirring occasionally, for 5 minutes, or until softened. Stir in the red and orange peppers, tomatoes with their juice, sun-dried tomato paste and paprika and bring to the boil.

Add the pepperoni and parsley and season to taste with salt and pepper. Stir well and bring to the boil, then reduce the heat and simmer for 10–15 minutes.

Meanwhile, bring a large, heavy-based saucepan of lightly salted water to the boil. Add the pasta, return to the boil and cook for 8–10 minutes, or according to the packet instructions, until tender but still firm to the bite. Drain well and transfer to a warmed serving dish. Add the remaining oil and toss to coat. Add the sauce and toss again. Sprinkle with parsley to garnish and serve immediately.

Parma Ham with Melon & Asparagus

serves 4

225 g/8 oz asparagus spears

1 small or ½ medium-sized Galia or cantaloupe melon

55 g/2 oz Parma ham, thinly sliced

150 g/5½ oz bag mixed salad leaves, such as herb salad with rocket

85 g/3 oz fresh raspberries

1 tbsp freshly shaved Parmesan cheese

for the dressing

1 tbsp balsamic vinegar

2 tbsp raspberry vinegar

2 tbsp orange juice

Trim the asparagus, cutting the spears in half if very long. Cook in lightly salted, boiling water over a medium heat for 5 minutes, or until tender. Drain and plunge into cold water then drain again and reserve.

Cut the melon in half and scoop out the seeds. Cut into small wedges and cut away the rind. Separate the Parma ham slices, cut in half and wrap around the melon wedges.

Arrange the salad leaves on a large serving platter and place the melon wedges on top together with the asparagus spears. Scatter over the raspberries and Parmesan shavings.

Pour the vinegars and juice into a screw-top jar and shake until blended. Pour over the salad and serve.

Chicken Morsels Fried in Batter

serves 6–8

500 g/1 lb 2 oz skinless, boneless chicken thighs

3 tbsp olive oil

juice of ½ lemon

2 garlic cloves, crushed

8 tbsp flour

vegetable oil for deep-frying

2 eggs, beaten

salt and pepper

fresh flat-leaf parsley sprigs, to garnish

lemon wedges, to serve

Cut the chicken thighs into 4-cm/1½-inch chunks. Mix the olive oil, lemon juice, garlic, salt and pepper in a bowl. Add the chicken pieces and leave to marinate at room temperature for an hour, or overnight in the refrigerator. Spread the flour on a plate and mix with a pinch of salt and plenty of black pepper.

When ready to cook, remove the chicken pieces from the marinade and drain.

Heat the vegetable oil in a deep-fat fryer or large saucepan to 180°C/350°F, or until a cube of bread browns in 30 seconds. Working in batches, roll the chicken pieces in the seasoned flour and then in beaten egg. Immediately drop into the hot oil, and deep-fry for about 5 minutes, until golden and crisp, turning occasionally with tongs. Drain on crumpled kitchen paper.

Place the chicken pieces in a warm serving dish and dress with parsley. Serve hot with thick wedges of lemon.

Minced Chicken Skewers

makes 8

450 g/1 lb fresh chicken mince

1 onion, finely chopped

1 fresh red chilli, deseeded and chopped

2 tbsp Thai red curry paste

1 tsp palm sugar or soft light brown sugar

1 tsp ground coriander

1 tsp ground cumin

1 egg white

8 lemon grass stalks

rice with chopped spring onion, to serve

coriander sprigs, to garnish

Mix the chicken, onion, chilli, curry paste and sugar together in a bowl to a thick paste. Stir in the coriander, cumin and egg white and mix again.

Preheat the grill to high. Divide the mixture into 8 equal portions and squeeze each one around a lemon grass stalk. Arrange on a grill rack and cook under the preheated grill, turning frequently, for 8 minutes, or until browned and cooked through. Serve immediately, accompanied by cooked rice with chopped spring onion stirred through it. Garnish with the coriander sprigs.

Quick Chicken Laksa

serves 4

850 ml/1½ pints canned coconut milk

200 ml/7 fl oz chicken stock

2–3 tbsp laksa paste

3 skinless, boneless chicken breasts, about 175 g/6 oz each, sliced into strips

250 g/9 oz cherry tomatoes, halved

250 g/9 oz mangetout, diagonally halved

200 g/7 oz dried rice noodles

1 bunch fresh coriander, roughly chopped

Pour the coconut milk and stock into a saucepan and stir in the laksa paste. Add the chicken strips and simmer for 10–15 minutes over a gentle heat until the chicken is cooked through.

Stir in the tomatoes, mangetout and noodles. Simmer for a further 2–3 minutes. Stir in the coriander and serve immediately.

Turkey Wraps with Brie & Cranberry

makes 4

4 x 25-cm/10-inch wraps

55 g/2 oz cranberry sauce

255 g/9 oz cooked turkey breast, shredded

150 g/5½ oz brie, sliced

salt and pepper

Preheat a non-stick pan or griddle pan until almost smoking, then cook the wraps one at a time on each side for 10 seconds. This will add some colour and also soften the wraps.

Spread the cranberry sauce over the wraps and divide the turkey and brie between the wraps, placing in the middle of each wrap. Sprinkle with salt and pepper and then fold in the ends. Roll up, cut in half on an angle and serve.

Turkey Ciabatta with Walnuts

serves 2

2 ciabatta rolls

100 g/4 oz blue cheese, such as Stilton or Danish blue, finely diced or crumbled

100 g/4 oz walnuts, chopped

8 large fresh sage leaves, finely shredded

4 slices cooked turkey breast

seedless green grapes, to serve

Preheat the grill to a medium–high setting. Slice the ciabatta rolls in half horizontally and toast the cut sides on the rack in the grill pan. Remove the top halves. Turn the bottom halves over and toast the undersides until brown and crisp. When the breads are toasted, set them aside and reduce the heat to a low setting.

Meanwhile, mix the blue cheese, walnuts and sage. Lay 2 turkey slices on the base of each roll and top with the cheese and walnut mixture, piling it up in the middle. Cover with the top of the roll.

Heat the rolls under the grill, well away from the heat, for 3–4 minutes, until the breads are hot and the cheese is beginning to melt. Increase the heat slightly, if necessary, to medium but do not turn it up high enough to brown the tops of the rolls before they are warmed through.

Serve the hot rolls with green grapes as an accompaniment.

Fish &
Seafood

Batter-Fried Fish Sticks

serves 6

115 g/4 oz plain flour, plus extra for dusting

pinch of salt

1 egg, beaten

1 tbsp Spanish olive oil

150 ml/5 fl oz water

600 g/1 lb 5 oz firm-fleshed white fish fillet, such as monkfish or hake

sunflower or olive oil, for deep-frying

lemon wedges, to serve

To make the batter, put the flour and salt into a large bowl and make a well in the centre. Pour the egg and olive oil into the well, then gradually add the water, mixing in the flour from the side and beating constantly, until all the flour is incorporated and a smooth batter forms.

Cut the fish into fingers about 2 cm/3/4 inch wide and 5 cm/ 2 inches long. Dust lightly with flour so that the batter sticks to them when they are dipped. Heat enough sunflower or olive oil for deep-frying in a deep-fat fryer to 180°C/350°F, or until a cube of bread browns in 30 seconds. Spear a fish stick onto a cocktail stick, dip into the batter and then drop the fish and cocktail stick into the hot oil.

Cook the fish sticks, in batches to avoid overcrowding, for 5 minutes, or until golden brown. Remove with a slotted spoon or draining basket and drain on kitchen paper. Keep hot in a warm oven while cooking the remaining fish sticks. Serve the fish sticks hot, with lemon wedges for squeezing over.

Salmon with Lemon & Olive Dressing

serves 4

2 tbsp olive oil

4 salmon fillets, skin on, about 175 g/6 oz each

juice of ½ lemon

salt

freshly boiled new potatoes and green salad, to serve

for the dressing

1 handful fresh basil leaves

2 tbsp snipped fresh chives

1 garlic clove, crushed

1 tsp wholegrain mustard

½ tsp caster sugar

juice of ½ lemon

200 ml/7 fl oz extra virgin olive oil

rind of ½ preserved lemon, finely chopped

10 pitted black olives, finely chopped

Preheat the oven to 200°C/400°F/Gas Mark 6. To make the dressing, put the herbs, garlic, mustard, sugar, lemon juice and extra virgin olive oil in a blender or food processor and blend until smooth. Pour the mixture into a small saucepan, add the preserved lemon rind and olives and warm over a gentle heat.

Meanwhile, heat the olive oil in a frying pan over a medium heat, add the salmon fillets, skin-side down, and cook for 3 minutes, or until the skin is golden and crisp. Lay the fish in a roasting tin, skin-side up, squeeze over the lemon juice and season with a little salt.

Roast in the preheated oven for 5 minutes, or until the fish is just cooked through – the exact timing will depend on the thickness of the fillets. Serve immediately, with the dressing spooned over the fish, accompanied by new potatoes and a green salad.

Teriyaki Salmon Fillets with Chinese Noodles

serves 4

4 salmon fillets, about 200 g/7 oz each

125 ml/4 fl oz teriyaki marinade

1 shallot, sliced

2-cm/¾-inch piece fresh ginger, finely chopped

2 carrots, sliced

115 g/4 oz closed-cup mushrooms, sliced

1.2 litres/2 pints vegetable stock

250 g/9 oz dried medium egg noodles

115 g/4 oz frozen peas

175 g/6 oz Chinese leaves, shredded

4 spring onions, sliced

Wipe off any fish scales from the salmon skin. Arrange the salmon fillets, skin side up, in a dish just large enough to fit them in a single layer. Mix the teriyaki marinade with the shallot and ginger in a small bowl and pour over the salmon. Cover and leave to marinate in the refrigerator for at least 1 hour, turning the salmon over halfway through the marinating time.

Put the carrots, mushrooms and stock into a large saucepan. Arrange the salmon, skin side down, on a shallow baking tray. Pour the fish marinade into the pan of vegetables and stock and bring to the boil. Reduce the heat, cover and simmer for 10 minutes.

Meanwhile, preheat the grill to medium. Cook the salmon under the preheated grill for 10–15 minutes, depending on the thickness of the fillets, until the flesh turns pink and flakes easily. Remove from under the grill and keep warm. Add the noodles and peas to the stock and return to the boil. Reduce the heat, cover and simmer for 5 minutes, or until the noodles are tender. Stir in the Chinese leaves and spring onions and heat through for 1 minute.

Carefully drain off 300 ml/10 fl oz of the stock into a small heatproof jug and reserve. Drain and discard the remaining stock. Divide the noodles and vegetables between 4 warmed serving bowls and top each with a salmon fillet. Pour over the reserved stock and serve immediately.

Smoked Salmon Tagliatelle

serves 4

350 g/12 oz dried tagliatelle

2 tbsp olive oil

1 garlic clove, finely chopped

115 g/4 oz smoked salmon, cut into thin strips

55 g/2 oz rocket

salt and pepper

Bring a large, heavy-based saucepan of lightly salted water to the boil. Add the pasta, return to the boil and cook for 8–10 minutes, or until tender but still firm to the bite.

Just before the end of the cooking time, heat the olive oil in a heavy-based frying pan. Add the garlic and cook over a low heat, stirring constantly, for 1 minute. Do not allow the garlic to brown or it will taste bitter.

Add the salmon and rocket. Season to taste with pepper and cook, stirring constantly, for 1 minute. Remove the frying pan from the heat.

Drain the pasta and transfer to a warmed serving dish. Add the smoked salmon and rocket mixture, toss lightly and serve.

Swordfish Steaks with Lemon Dressing

serves 4

5 tbsp olive oil, plus extra
for brushing

juice of ½ large or
1 small lemon

2 garlic cloves,
well crushed

2 tsp finely chopped
fresh oregano

2 tbsp chopped
fresh parsley

4 swordfish steaks, about
175 g/6 oz each

salt and pepper

lemon wedges, to garnish

freshly cooked asparagus
to serve

Put all the ingredients, except the swordfish, including salt and pepper to taste, in a screw-top jar and shake well to combine.

Preheat a ridged griddle pan over a high heat. Pat the swordfish steaks dry with kitchen paper and lightly brush with oil on both sides. When the griddle pan is very hot, add the swordfish steaks and cook for 2 minutes on each side, or until cooked through but still moist inside.

Serve immediately, accompanied by freshly cooked asparagus and garnished with lemon wedges. Shake the lemon dressing again and drizzle it over the swordfish.

Crispy Parmesan-coated Sea Bass

serves 4

3 tbsp olive oil

4 sea bass fillets, about 125 g/4½ oz each, skin on and pin-boned

juice and grated rind of 1 lemon

100 g/3½ oz Parmesan cheese, finely grated

1 small bunch fresh parsley, finely chopped

salt and pepper

watercress, rocket or spinach salad and lemon wedges, to serve

Preheat the grill to its highest setting. Brush the grill pan with a little of the oil and lay the fillets in the grill pan, skin-side down. Drizzle over a little of the remaining oil, give each fillet a good squeeze of lemon juice and season with salt and pepper.

Mix the lemon rind, Parmesan cheese and parsley together and scatter evenly over the fish. Drizzle over the remaining oil. Cook under the grill for 4 minutes, or until the fish is just cooked and golden – the exact cooking time will depend on the thickness of the fillets. Serve immediately with a salad of watercress, rocket or spinach leaves and lemon wedges.

Lentil & Tuna Salad

serves 4

2 ripe tomatoes

1 small red onion

400 g/14 oz can
lentils, drained

185 g/6½ oz can
tuna, drained

2 tbsp chopped
fresh coriander

pepper

for the dressing

3 tbsp virgin olive oil

1 tbsp lemon juice

1 tsp wholegrain mustard

1 garlic clove, crushed

½ tsp ground cumin

½ tsp ground coriander

Using a sharp knife, deseed the tomatoes and then chop them into fine dice. Finely chop the red onion.

To make the dressing, whisk together the virgin olive oil, lemon juice, mustard, garlic, cumin and ground coriander in a small bowl until thoroughly combined. Set aside until required.

Mix together the chopped onion, diced tomatoes and drained lentils in a large bowl.

Flake the tuna with a fork and stir it into the onion, tomato and lentil mixture. Stir in the chopped fresh coriander and mix well.

Pour the dressing over the lentil and tuna salad and season with pepper to taste. Serve immediately.

Spicy Tuna Fishcakes

makes 4 fishcakes

4 tbsp plain flour

200 g/7 oz canned tuna in oil, drained

2–3 tbsp curry paste

1 spring onion, trimmed and finely chopped

1 egg, beaten

sunflower or groundnut oil, for frying

salt and pepper

rocket leaves, to serve

Mix the flour with plenty of salt and pepper on a large flat plate. Mash the tuna with the curry paste, spring onion and beaten egg in a large bowl.

Form into 4 patties and dust with the seasoned flour.

Heat the oil in a frying pan, add the patties and fry for 3–4 minutes on each side until crisp and golden. Serve on a bed of rocket leaves.

Prawn & Mango Salad

serves 4

2 mangoes

225 g/8 oz peeled, cooked prawns

salad leaves, to serve

4 whole cooked prawns, to garnish

for the dressing

juice from the mangoes

6 tbsp natural yogurt

2 tbsp mayonnaise

1 tbsp lemon juice

salt and pepper

Cutting close to the stone, cut a large slice from one side of each mango, then cut another slice from the opposite side. Without breaking the skin, cut the flesh in the segments into squares, then push the skin inside out to expose the cubes and cut away from the skin. Use a sharp knife to peel the remaining centre section of the mango and cut the flesh away from the stone into cubes. Reserve any juice in a bowl and put the mango flesh in a separate bowl.

Add the prawns to the mango flesh. Mix together the mango juice, yogurt, mayonnaise, lemon juice, salt and pepper until well blended.

Arrange the salad leaves on a serving dish and add the mango flesh and prawns. Pour over the dressing and serve garnished with the whole prawns.

Wok-fried King Prawns in Spicy Sauce

serves 4

3 tbsp vegetable or groundnut oil

450 g/1 lb raw king prawns, unpeeled

2 tsp finely chopped fresh ginger

1 tsp finely chopped garlic

1 tbsp chopped spring onion

2 tbsp chilli bean sauce

1 tsp Shaoxing rice wine

1 tsp sugar

½ tsp light soy sauce, plus extra to serve

1–2 tbsp chicken stock

Preheat a wok, heat the oil, then toss in the prawns and stir-fry over a high heat for about 4 minutes. Arrange the prawns on the sides of the wok, out of the oil, then add the ginger and garlic and stir until fragrant. Add the spring onion and chilli bean sauce. Stir the prawns into the mixture.

Reduce the heat slightly and add the rice wine, sugar, soy sauce and stock. Cover and cook for a further minute. Serve immediately, with extra soy sauce alongside.

Malaysian-style Coconut Noodles with Prawns

serves 4

2 tbsp vegetable oil

1 small red pepper, deseeded and diced

200 g/7 oz pak choi, stalks thinly sliced and leaves chopped

2 large garlic cloves, chopped

1 tsp ground turmeric

2 tsp garam masala

125 ml/4 fl oz hot vegetable stock

2 heaped tbsp smooth peanut butter

350 ml/12 fl oz coconut milk

1 tbsp tamari

250 g/9 oz dried rice noodles

280 g/10 oz large cooked and peeled prawns

2 spring onions, finely shredded, and 1 tbsp sesame seeds, to garnish

Heat the oil in a preheated wok or large, heavy-based frying pan over a high heat. Add the red pepper, pak choi stalks and garlic and stir-fry for 3 minutes. Add the turmeric, garam masala and pak choi leaves and stir-fry for a further minute.

Mix the hot stock and peanut butter together in a heatproof bowl until the peanut butter has dissolved, then add to the stir-fry with the coconut milk and tamari. Cook over a medium heat for 5 minutes, or until reduced and thickened.

Meanwhile, soak the noodles in a saucepan of just-boiled water for 3–4 minutes, or according to the packet instructions, until tender, then drain the noodles and refresh under cold running water. Add the noodles and prawns to the curry and cook, stirring frequently, for a further 2–3 minutes until heated through.

Serve the noodle dish immediately, sprinkled with the shredded spring onions and sesame seeds.

Prawn Toasts

makes 16

100 g/3½ oz raw prawns,
peeled and deveined

2 egg whites

2 tbsp cornflour

½ tsp sugar

pinch of salt

2 tbsp finely chopped fresh
coriander leaves

2 slices day-old
white bread

vegetable or groundnut oil,
for deep-frying

Pound the prawns to a pulp in a mortar with a pestle or with the base of a cleaver.

Mix the prawns with one of the egg whites and half the cornflour in a bowl. Add the sugar and salt, and stir in the coriander. Mix the remaining egg white with the remaining cornflour in a jug.

Remove the crusts from the bread and cut each slice into 8 triangles. Brush the top of each piece with the egg white and cornflour mixture, then add 1 teaspoon of the prawn mixture and spread smoothly over the top.

Heat enough oil for deep-frying in a wok, deep-fat fryer or large, heavy-based saucepan to 180°C/350°F, or until a cube of bread browns in 30 seconds. Without overcrowding the pan, cook the toasts prawn-side up for 2 minutes. Turn and cook for a further 2 minutes until beginning to turn golden brown. Remove with a slotted spoon, drain on kitchen paper and keep warm in a low oven while cooking the remainder.

Crab Fritters with Avocado Salsa

serves 4

200 g/7 oz lightly cooked sweetcorn kernels

70 g/2½ oz plain flour

2 eggs, beaten

300 g/10½ oz fresh or canned white crabmeat

1 small bunch fresh parsley, chopped

3–4 tbsp olive oil

salt and pepper

lime wedges, to serve

for the avocado salsa

1 small red onion, finely chopped

1 red pepper

1 yellow pepper

1 avocado

1 mango

4 tomatoes

juice and finely grated rind of 2 limes

1 large bunch fresh coriander, chopped

First make the salsa. Put the onion in a bowl. Remove the stalks and seeds from the peppers, and cut the flesh into 1-cm/½-inch dice. Add to the onion. Peel the avocado and mango, remove the stones and cut the flesh into 1-cm/½-inch dice. Add to the bowl. Chop the tomatoes into 1-cm/½-inch dice and add to the other ingredients. Stir in the lime juice and rind and coriander. Season to taste with salt and pepper.

Put the sweetcorn kernels, flour and eggs in a separate bowl and stir until well mixed. Lightly fold in the crabmeat and parsley, and season to taste with salt and pepper.

Heat the oil in a large frying pan over a medium-high heat. Drop spoonfuls of the batter into the hot oil and cook in batches for 2–3 minutes on each side until crisp and golden. Remove and drain on kitchen paper. Serve immediately with the salsa and the lime wedges.

Crab & Fennel Wraps

makes 4

250 g/9 oz baby fennel

150 g/5½ oz fresh or canned white crabmeat

4 tbsp mayonnaise

zest and juice of 1 lemon

small bunch of fresh flat-leaf parsley, shredded

4 x 25-cm/10-inch Mediterranean herb wraps

salt and pepper

Cut the fennel in half lengthways and then slice thinly.

Place the sliced fennel in a bowl with the crabmeat, mayonnaise, lemon zest and juice, parsley, salt and pepper. Mix well.

Leave for 5 minutes to allow the lemon juice to wilt the fennel slightly.

Preheat a non-stick pan or griddle pan until almost smoking, then cook the wraps one at a time on each side for 10 seconds. This will add some colour and also soften the wraps.

Give the filling mixture another stir and then divide between the wraps, placing one portion in the middle of each wrap. Fold in the ends, roll up, cut in half at an angle and serve.

Crab Cake Toasts

makes 8

3 slices good white bread, crusts removed

2 tbsp milk

55 g/2 oz butter, melted

170 g/6 oz fresh or canned white crabmeat

1 green chilli, deseeded and chopped

1 spring onion, finely chopped

salt and pepper

lemon wedges, to serve

Place one piece of bread on a plate and spoon the milk evenly over it. Leave to stand for a few minutes. Brush the remaining slices lightly on both sides with butter.

Mix the crabmeat, chilli and spring onion in a bowl. Mash the soaked bread with a fork and mix it with the crabmeat, scraping in the milk off the plate. Stir in the remaining melted butter and seasoning to taste.

Preheat the grill to a medium–high setting and toast the buttered bread on the rack in the grill pan, until crisp and golden on both sides. Top with the crab mixture, spreading it evenly right over the edges and forking the surface slightly so that it is not too smooth.

Place under the grill for about 3 minutes, until the creamy topping is browned. Cut into quarters and serve at once with lemon wedges for squeezing over the crab.

Wine-steamed Mussels

serves 4

2 kg/4 lb 8 oz live mussels, scrubbed and beards removed

115 g/4 oz butter

1 shallot, chopped

3 garlic cloves, finely chopped

225 ml/8 fl oz dry white wine

½ tsp salt

pepper

4 tbsp chopped fresh parsley

Discard any mussels that refuse to close when tapped. Melt half the butter in a very large saucepan over a low heat. Add the shallot and garlic and cook for 2 minutes. Add the mussels, wine, salt and a sprinkling of pepper.

Cover, bring to the boil, then boil for 3 minutes, shaking the pan from time to time.

Remove the mussels from the pan with a slotted spoon and place in individual serving bowls. Discard any mussels that remain closed.

Mix the remaining butter with the parsley in a small bowl and stir the mixture into the cooking juices in the pan. Bring to the boil and pour over the mussels. Serve immediately.

Pancetta-wrapped Scallops

serves 4

8 slices pancetta, halved

1 tbsp olive oil

juice of 1 lemon

pepper

16 scallops, prepared

lemon wedges, to serve

Preheat the grill. Wrap each scallop in half a slice of pancetta. Mix the oil, lemon juice and a sprinkling of black pepper together in a bowl.

Coat the scallops in the mixture and thread onto metal skewers (4 on each skewer). Discard any leftover lemon juice mixture.

Cook the scallops under a medium–hot grill for 4–5 minutes, turning once until cooked. Serve immediately with lemon wedges.

3

Vegetarian

Nachos

serves 6

175 g/6 oz tortilla chips

400 g/14 oz canned refried beans, warmed

2 tbsp finely chopped bottled jalapeño chillies

200 g/7 oz canned or bottled pimentos or roasted peppers, drained and finely sliced

salt and pepper

115 g/4 oz Gruyère cheese, grated

115 g/4 oz Cheddar cheese, grated

Preheat the oven to 200°C/400°F/Gas Mark 6.

Spread the tortilla chips out over the base of a large, shallow, ovenproof dish or roasting tin. Cover with the warmed refried beans. Scatter over the chillies and pimentos and season to taste with salt and pepper. Mix the cheeses together in a bowl and sprinkle on top.

Bake in the preheated oven for 5–8 minutes, or until the cheese is bubbling and melted. Serve immediately.

Hummus with Crudités

serves 4

175 g/6 oz canned chickpeas

125 ml/4 fl oz tahini

2 garlic cloves

125 ml/4 fl oz lemon juice

2–3 tbsp water

1 tbsp olive oil

1 tbsp chopped fresh parsley

pinch of cayenne pepper

salt

for the crudités

selection of vegetables, including carrots, cauliflower and celery

Drain and rinse the chickpeas. Place them in a blender or food processor with the tahini, garlic and lemon juice and season to taste with salt. Process, gradually adding the water, until smooth and creamy.

Scrape the chickpea mixture into a serving bowl and make a hollow in the centre. Pour the olive oil into the hollow and sprinkle with the chopped fresh parsley and the cayenne pepper.

Slice the raw vegetables into bite-sized portions and arrange on a large serving platter. Serve with the hummus.

Warm Pasta Salad

serves 4

225 g/8 oz dried farfalle or other pasta shapes

6 pieces sun-dried tomato in oil, drained and chopped

4 spring onions, chopped

55 g/2 oz rocket leaves

½ cucumber, deseeded and diced

salt and pepper

for the dressing

4 tbsp olive oil

1 tbsp white wine vinegar

½ tsp caster sugar

1 tsp Dijon mustard

salt and pepper

4 fresh basil leaves, finely shredded

To make the dressing, whisk the olive oil, vinegar, sugar and mustard together in a jug. Season to taste with salt and pepper and stir in the basil.

Bring a large, heavy-based saucepan of lightly salted water to the boil. Add the pasta, return to the boil and cook for 8–10 minutes, or until tender but still firm to the bite. Drain and transfer to a salad bowl. Add the dressing and toss well.

Add the tomatoes, spring onions, rocket and cucumber, season to taste with salt and pepper and toss. Serve warm.

Fusilli with Gorgonzola & Mushroom Sauce

serves 4

350 g/12 oz dried fusilli

3 tbsp olive oil

350 g/12 oz wild mushrooms, sliced

1 garlic clove, finely chopped

400 ml/14 fl oz double cream

250 g/9 oz Gorgonzola cheese, crumbled

salt and pepper

2 tbsp chopped fresh flat-leaf parsley, to garnish

green salad, to serve

Bring a large saucepan of lightly salted water to the boil. Add the pasta, return to the boil and cook according to the packet instructions until tender but still firm to the bite.

Meanwhile, heat the oil in a large, heavy-based saucepan over a low heat. Add the mushrooms and cook, stirring frequently, for 5 minutes. Add the garlic and cook, stirring, for a further 2 minutes.

Add the cream, bring to the boil and cook for 1 minute until slightly thickened. Stir in the cheese and cook over a low heat until it has melted. Do not allow the sauce to boil once the cheese has been added. Season to taste with salt and pepper and remove from the heat.

Drain the pasta and add to the sauce. Toss well to coat, then serve immediately, garnished with the parsley, and accompanied by a green salad.

Pasta with Chicory & Walnuts

serves 4

3 tbsp olive oil

2 garlic cloves, crushed

3 heads chicory, sliced

1 tbsp runny honey

100 g/3½ fl oz walnuts

450 g/1 lb dried penne pasta

salt and pepper

Heat the oil in a frying pan over a low heat, add the garlic and chicory and cook, stirring, for 3–4 minutes until the chicory begins to wilt. Stir in the honey and walnuts and cook, stirring occasionally, for a further 4–5 minutes. Season to taste with salt and pepper.

Meanwhile, cook the pasta in a large saucepan of lightly salted boiling water according to the packet instructions until tender but still firm to the bite. Drain and toss with the chicory mixture. Serve immediately.

Pear & Roquefort Open Sandwiches

serves 2–4

4 slices walnut bread or pain Poilâne, about 1 cm/½ inch thick

2 ripe pears, such as Conference, peeled, halved, cored and thinly sliced lengthways

100 g/3½ oz Roquefort cheese, very thinly sliced

Preheat the grill to a medium–high setting. Toast the bread slices on the rack in the grill pan until crisp, but not brown, on both sides. Do not turn off the grill.

Divide the pear slices equally between the breads. Lay the cheese slices on top.

Return the breads to the grill until the cheese melts and bubbles. Serve.

Green Olive Hummus Wraps

makes 4

4 x 25-cm/10-inch wraps

4 cherry tomatoes, halved

½ cucumber, deseeded and quartered

55 g/2 oz baby spinach leaves

for the hummus

200 g/7 oz canned chickpeas, drained

1 clove garlic, crushed

4 tbsp extra virgin olive oil

1 tsp tahini

1 tsp lemon juice

55 g/2 oz stoned green olives, chopped, plus whole olives, to garnish

small bunch of flat-leaf parsley, shredded

salt and pepper

To make the hummus place the chickpeas, garlic, olive oil, tahini and lemon juice in a food processor and blend until smooth. Season with salt and pepper. Scrape into a bowl and mix in the olives and parsley.

Preheat a non-stick pan or grill pan until almost smoking, then cook the wraps one at a time on each side for 10 seconds. This will add some colour and also soften the wraps.

Spread the hummus over the wraps and divide the cherry tomatoes, cucumber and spinach between them, placing a portion in the middle of each wrap. Fold in at the ends, roll up, cut in half and serve, garnished with the whole olives.

Wild Garlic & Broccoli Crostini

serves 6

500 g/1 lb 2 oz broccoli, stems trimmed and cut into lengths short enough to fit on the crostini

100 ml/3½ fl oz olive oil

1 small bunch wild garlic, rinsed, patted dry and chopped

1–2 red chillies, deseeded and finely chopped

6 slices good-quality country-style bread

salt and pepper

Preheat the oven to 190°C/375°F/Gas Mark 5.

Cook the broccoli in a large saucepan of salted water for 10 minutes, or until just tender. Drain well and set aside.

Heat about one third of the oil in a wok or large frying pan over a high heat, add the wild garlic and chilli and stir-fry for 2 minutes. Add the broccoli, season to taste with salt and pepper and stir-fry for 3–4 minutes until hot and crisp.

Meanwhile, drizzle the remaining oil evenly over the bread slices and bake in the preheated oven for 10 minutes, or until crisp and golden.

Divide the broccoli mixture between the crostini, add a grinding of pepper, and serve immediately.

Cheese & Sun-Dried Tomato Toasts

serves 4

2 sfilatini

175 ml/6 fl oz sun-dried tomato purée

300 g/10½ oz mozzarella, drained and diced

1½ tsp dried oregano

2–3 tbsp olive oil

pepper

Preheat the oven to 220°C/425°F/Gas Mark 7.

Slice the loaves diagonally and discard the end pieces. Toast the slices on both sides under a preheated grill until golden.

Spread one side of each toast with the sun-dried tomato purée and top with mozzarella. Sprinkle with oregano and season to taste with pepper.

Place the toasts on a large baking sheet and drizzle with olive oil. Bake in the preheated oven, for about 5 minutes, until the cheese has melted and is bubbling. Remove the hot toasts from the oven and leave them to stand for 5 minutes before serving.

Eggs & Peppers on Toast

serves 4

2 tbsp olive oil

2 large red peppers, deseeded and chopped

1 small red onion, very finely chopped

pinch of paprika, plus extra to garnish (optional)

4 slices dark rye bread

8 large organic eggs

4 tbsp milk

salt and pepper

Heat half the oil in a non-stick frying pan over a medium–high heat, add the red peppers and onion and cook, stirring frequently, for 10 minutes, or until soft. Add the paprika, stir and set aside.

Toast one side of the bread slices. Brush the other sides with 1 tablespoon of the remaining oil, then lightly toast. Keep warm.

Beat the eggs with the milk and a little salt and pepper to taste in a bowl. Brush the remaining oil over the base of a non-stick saucepan, add the egg mixture and cook over a medium–high heat, stirring frequently to make sure that the eggs don't stick, for 5 minutes, or until cooked to your liking.

Gently stir in the red pepper mixture, then spoon onto the rye toasts. Sprinkle with a little extra paprika to garnish, if you like, and serve immediately.

Mixed Herb Omelette

serves 1

2 large eggs

2 tbsp milk

40 g/1½ oz butter

1 fresh flat-leaf parsley sprig, stem bruised

leaves from 1 fresh flat-leaf parsley sprig

1 fresh chervil sprig

2 fresh chives, chopped

salt and pepper

fresh salad leaves, to serve

Break the eggs into a bowl. Add the milk and salt and pepper to taste, and quickly beat until just blended.

Heat a 20-cm/8-inch omelette pan or frying pan over a medium–high heat until very hot and you can feel the heat rising from the surface. Add 25 g/1 oz of the butter and use a spatula to rub it over the base and around the side of the pan as it melts.

As soon as the butter stops sizzling, pour in the eggs. Shake the pan forwards and backwards over the heat and use the spatula to stir the eggs around the pan in a circular motion. Do not scrape the base of the pan.

As the omelette begins to set, use the spatula to push the cooked egg from the edge towards the centre, so that the remaining uncooked egg comes in contact with the hot base of the pan. Continue doing this for 3 minutes, or until the omelette looks set on the bottom but is still slightly runny on top.

Put the herbs in the centre of the omelette. Tilt the pan away from the handle, so that the omelette slides towards the edge of the pan. Use the spatula to fold the top half of the omelette over the herbs. Slide the omelette onto a plate, then rub the remaining butter over the top. Serve immediately, accompanied by fresh salad leaves.

Mozzarella Salad with Sun-dried Tomatoes

serves 4

100 g/3½ oz mixed salad leaves, such as oakleaf lettuce, baby spinach and rocket

500 g/1 lb 2 oz smoked mozzarella, sliced

for the dressing

140 g/5 oz sun-dried tomatoes in olive oil (drained weight), reserving the oil from the bottle

15 g/½ oz fresh basil, coarsely shredded

15 g/½ oz fresh flat-leaf parsley, coarsely chopped

1 tbsp capers, rinsed

1 tbsp balsamic vinegar

1 garlic clove, coarsely chopped

extra olive oil, if necessary

pepper

Put the sun-dried tomatoes, basil, parsley, capers, vinegar and garlic in a food processor or blender. Measure the oil from the sun-dried tomatoes jar and make it up to 150 ml/5 fl oz with more olive oil if necessary. Add it to the food processor or blender and process until smooth. Season to taste with pepper.

Divide the salad leaves between 4 individual serving plates. Top with the slices of mozzarella and spoon the dressing over them. Serve immediately.

Raspberry & Feta Salad with Couscous

serves 6

350 g/12 oz couscous

600 ml/1 pint boiling vegetable stock

350 g/12 oz fresh raspberries

small bunch of fresh basil

225 g/8 oz feta cheese, cubed or crumbled

2 courgettes, thinly sliced

4 spring onions, trimmed and diagonally sliced

55 g/2 oz pine kernels, toasted

grated rind of 1 lemon

for the dressing

1 tbsp white wine vinegar

1 tbsp balsamic vinegar

4 tbsp extra virgin olive oil

juice of 1 lemon

salt and pepper

Put the couscous in a large, heatproof bowl and pour over the stock. Stir well, cover and leave to soak until all the stock has been absorbed.

Pick over the raspberries, discarding any that are overripe. Shred the basil leaves.

Transfer the couscous to a large serving bowl and stir well to break up any lumps. Add the cheese, courgettes, spring onions, raspberries and pine kernels. Stir in the basil and lemon rind and gently toss all the ingredients together.

Put all the dressing ingredients in a screw-top jar, screw on the lid and shake until well blended. Pour over the salad and serve.

Crispy Spring Rolls

makes 8

2 tbsp vegetable or groundnut oil, plus extra for deep-frying

6 spring onions, cut into 5-cm/2-inch lengths

1 fresh green chilli, deseeded and chopped

1 carrot, cut into thin batons

1 courgette, cut into thin batons

1/2 red pepper, deseeded and thinly sliced

115 g/4 oz beansprouts, drained and rinsed if canned

115 g/4 oz canned bamboo shoots, drained and rinsed

3 tbsp Thai soy sauce

1–2 tbsp chilli sauce

8 spring roll wrappers

Heat the oil in a preheated wok or large frying pan over a high heat. Add the spring onions and chilli and stir-fry for 30 seconds. Add the carrot, courgette and red pepper and stir-fry for 1 minute. Remove from heat and stir in the beansprouts, bamboo shoots, soy sauce and chilli sauce.

Taste and add more soy sauce or chilli sauce if necessary. Lay a spring roll wrapper on a work surface and spoon some of the vegetable mixture diagonally across the centre. Roll one corner over the filling and flip the sides of the wrapper over the top, to enclose the filling. Continue to roll up to make an enclosed parcel. Repeat with the remaining wrappers and filling to make 8 spring rolls.

Heat the oil for deep-frying in a preheated wok or large frying pan to 180°C/350°F, or until a cube of bread browns in 30 seconds. Add the spring rolls, in 2 batches, and cook until crisp and golden brown. Remove with a slotted spoon, drain on kitchen paper and keep the first batch hot while you cook the remaining spring rolls, then serve immediately.

Tofu Stir-fry

serves 4

2 tbsp sunflower or olive oil

350 g/12 oz firm tofu, cubed

225 g/8 oz pak choi, roughly chopped

1 garlic clove, chopped

4 tbsp sweet chilli sauce

2 tbsp light soy sauce

Heat 1 tablespoon of oil in a wok, add the tofu in batches and stir-fry for 2–3 minutes until golden. Remove and set aside.

Add the pak choi to the wok and stir-fry for a few seconds until tender and wilted. Remove and set aside.

Add the remaining oil to the wok, then add the garlic and stir-fry for 30 seconds.

Stir in the chilli sauce and soy sauce and bring to the boil.

Return the tofu and pak choi to the wok and toss gently until coated in the sauce. Serve immediately.

Filo-wrapped Asparagus

serves 4

20 asparagus spears

5 sheets filo pastry

lemon wedges, to serve

for the dip

85 g/3 oz natural cottage cheese

1 tbsp semi-skimmed milk

4 spring onions, trimmed and finely chopped

2 tbsp chopped fresh mixed herbs, such as basil, mint and tarragon

pepper

Preheat the oven to 190°C/375°F/Gas Mark 5. To make the dip, put the cottage cheese in a bowl and add the milk. Beat until smooth, then stir in the spring onions, chopped herbs and pepper to taste. Place in a serving bowl, cover lightly and chill in the refrigerator until required.

Cut off and discard the woody end of the asparagus and shave with a vegetable peeler to remove any woody parts from the spears.

Cut the filo pastry into quarters and place one sheet on a work surface. Brush lightly with water then place a spear at one end. Roll up to encase the spear, and place on a large baking sheet. Repeat until all the asparagus spears are wrapped in pastry.

Bake for 10–12 minutes, or until the pastry is golden. Serve the spears with lemon wedges and the dip on the side.

Asparagus with Lemon Butter Sauce

serves 4

800 g/1 lb 12 oz asparagus
spears, trimmed

1 tbsp olive oil

salt and pepper

for the sauce

juice of ½ lemon

2 tbsp water

100 g/3½ oz butter, cut
into cubes

Preheat the oven to 200°C/400°F/Gas Mark 6. Lay the asparagus spears out in a single layer on a large baking sheet. Drizzle over the oil, season to taste with salt and pepper and roast in the preheated oven for 10 minutes, or until just tender.

Meanwhile, make the sauce. Pour the lemon juice into a saucepan and add the water. Heat for a minute or so, then slowly add the butter, cube by cube, stirring constantly until it has all been incorporated. Season to taste with pepper and serve immediately, drizzled over the asparagus.

Creamed Mushrooms

serves 4

juice of 1 small lemon

450 g/1 lb small button mushrooms

25 g/1 oz butter

1 tbsp sunflower or olive oil

1 small onion, finely chopped

125 ml/4 fl oz whipping or double cream

salt and pepper

1 tbsp chopped fresh parsley, plus 4 sprigs, to garnish

Sprinkle a little of the lemon juice over the mushrooms.

Heat the butter and oil in a frying pan, add the onion and cook for 1 minute. Add the mushrooms, shaking the pan so they do not stick.

Season to taste with salt and pepper, then stir in the cream, chopped parsley and remaining lemon juice.

Heat until hot but do not allow to boil, then transfer to a serving plate and garnish with the parsley sprigs. Serve immediately.

4

Desserts

Quick Tiramisù

serves 4

225 g/8 oz mascarpone
cheese or full-fat
soft cheese

1 egg, separated

2 tbsp natural yogurt

2 tbsp caster sugar

2 tbsp dark rum

2 tbsp cold strong
black coffee

8 sponge fingers

2 tbsp grated plain
chocolate

Put the mascarpone cheese, egg yolk and yogurt in a large bowl and beat together until smooth.

Whisk the egg white in a separate, spotlessly clean, grease-free bowl until stiff but not dry, then whisk in the sugar and gently fold into the cheese mixture. Divide half the mixture between 4 sundae glasses.

Mix the rum and coffee together in a shallow dish. Dip the sponge fingers into the rum mixture, break them in half, or into smaller pieces if necessary, and divide between the glasses.

Stir any remaining coffee mixture into the remaining cheese mixture and divide between the glasses. Sprinkle with the grated chocolate. Serve immediately or cover and chill in the refrigerator until required.

White Chocolate Brownies

makes 8

115 g/4 oz butter, plus extra for greasing

225 g/8 oz white chocolate

75 g/2¾ oz walnut pieces

2 eggs

115 g/4 oz soft brown sugar

115 g/4 oz self-raising flour

Preheat the oven to 180°C/350°F/Gas Mark 4. Lightly grease an 18-cm/7-inch square cake tin.

Roughly chop the chocolate and walnuts. Put 175 g/6 oz of the chocolate and the butter in a heatproof bowl set over a saucepan of gently simmering water. When melted, stir together, then set aside to cool slightly.

Whisk the eggs and sugar together, then beat in the cooled chocolate mixture until well mixed. Fold in the flour, chopped chocolate and walnuts. Turn the mixture into the prepared tin and smooth the surface.

Transfer the tin to the preheated oven and bake the brownies for about 30 minutes, until just set. The mixture should still be a little soft in the centre. Leave to cool in the tin, then cut into rectangles or squares before serving.

Chocolate Chip Flapjack

makes 12

115 g/4 oz butter, plus extra
for greasing

60 g/2¼ oz caster sugar

1 tbsp golden syrup

350 g/12 oz rolled oats

85 g/3 oz plain
chocolate chips

85 g/3 oz sultanas

Preheat the oven to 180°C/350°F/Gas Mark 4. Lightly grease a 20-cm/8-inch square, shallow cake tin.

Place the butter, caster sugar and golden syrup in a saucepan and cook over a low heat, stirring constantly, until the butter and sugar melt and the mixture is well combined.

Remove the saucepan from the heat and stir in the rolled oats until they are well coated. Add the chocolate chips and the sultanas and mix well to combine everything.

Turn into the prepared tin and press down well.
Bake in the preheated oven for 30 minutes. Cool slightly, then mark into squares. When almost cold, cut into squares and transfer to a wire rack to cool completely.

Marshmallow Muffin

makes 12

70 g/2½ oz butter

280 g/10 oz plain flour

6 tbsp cocoa powder

3 tsp baking powder

85 g/3 oz caster sugar

1 egg, beaten

300 ml/10 fl oz milk

100 g/3½ oz milk chocolate chips

55 g/2 oz white mini marshmallows

Preheat the oven to 190°C/375°F/Gas Mark 5. Place 12 muffin paper cases in a muffin tin. Melt the butter.

Sift the flour, cocoa and baking powder together into a large bowl. Stir in the sugar.

Whisk the egg, milk and melted butter together, then gently stir into the flour mixture to form a stiff batter. Gently stir in the chocolate chips and marshmallows. Spoon the mixture into the muffin cases.

Bake the muffins in the preheated oven for 20–25 minutes, until well risen. Leave to cool in the tin for 5 minutes, then transfer to a wire rack and leave to cool completely.

Chocolate Ice-cream Bites

serves 6

600 ml/1 pint good-quality ice cream

200 g/7 oz plain chocolate

2 tbsp unsalted butter

Line a baking tray with clingfilm.

Using a melon baller, scoop out balls of ice cream and place them on the prepared baking tray. Alternatively, cut the ice cream into bite-size cubes. Stick a cocktail stick in each piece and return to the freezer until very hard.

Place the chocolate and the butter in a heatproof bowl set over a saucepan of gently simmering water until melted. Quickly dip the frozen ice-cream balls into the warm chocolate and return to the freezer. Keep them there until ready to serve.

Chocolate Zabaglione

serves 4

4 egg yolks

4 tbsp caster sugar

50 g/1¾ oz finely grated plain chocolate

125 ml/4 fl oz Marsala

cocoa powder, for dusting

amaretti biscuits, to serve (optional)

Put the egg yolks and sugar in a large heatproof bowl and whisk together using a hand-held electric whisk until very pale.

Fold the chocolate into the egg mixture.

Gradually fold the Marsala into the chocolate mixture. Set the bowl over a saucepan of gently simmering water and set the electric whisk on the lowest speed or use a balloon whisk. Cook gently, whisking constantly, until the mixture thickens; take care not to overcook or the mixture will curdle.

Spoon the hot mixture into warmed individual glass dishes or coffee cups and dust with cocoa powder. Serve the zabaglione as soon as possible so that it is warm, light and fluffy, accompanied by amaretti biscuits, if you like.

Chocolate Banana Sundae

serves 4

150 ml/5 fl oz double cream

4 bananas

8–12 scoops good-quality
vanilla ice cream

75 g/2¾ oz flaked or
chopped almonds,
toasted

grated or flaked chocolate,
for sprinkling

4 fan wafers, to serve

glossy chocolate sauce

55 g/2 oz plain chocolate,
broken into small pieces

4 tbsp golden syrup

1 tbsp butter

1 tbsp brandy or dark rum
(optional)

To make the chocolate sauce, put the chocolate, syrup and butter in a heatproof bowl set over a saucepan of barely simmering water. Heat, stirring, until melted and smooth. Remove the bowl from the heat and stir in the brandy, if using.

Whip the cream in a separate bowl until it is just holding its shape. Peel and slice the bananas. Put a scoop of ice cream in the bottom of each of 4 tall sundae dishes. Top with slices of banana, some chocolate sauce, a spoonful of the whipped cream and a generous sprinkling of nuts.

Repeat the layers, finishing with a good dollop of whipped cream, a sprinkling of nuts and a little grated chocolate. Serve with fan wafers.

Chocolate Popcorn

makes about 250 g/9 oz

3 tbsp sunflower oil

70 g/2½ oz popcorn

25 g/1 oz butter

55 g/2 oz light soft brown sugar

2 tbsp golden syrup

1 tbsp milk

55 g/2 oz plain chocolate chips

Preheat the oven to 150°C/300°F/Gas Mark 2. Heat the oil in a large, heavy-based saucepan. Add the popcorn, cover the saucepan, and cook, shaking the saucepan vigorously and frequently, for about 2 minutes, until the popping stops. Turn the popcorn into a large bowl.

Put the butter, sugar, golden syrup and milk in a saucepan and heat gently until the butter has melted. Bring to the boil, without stirring, and boil for 2 minutes. Remove from the heat, add the chocolate chips, and stir until melted.

Pour the chocolate mixture over the popcorn and toss together until evenly coated. Spread the mixture onto a large baking tray.

Bake the popcorn in the oven for about 15 minutes, until crisp. Leave to cool before serving.

Mocha Fondue

serves 4

250 g/9 oz plain chocolate (at least 50% cocoa solids), broken into small pieces

100 ml/3½ fl oz double cream

1 tbsp instant coffee granules

3 tbsp coffee-flavoured liqueur, such as Kahlúa

for the dippers

small sweet biscuits, such as amaretti

plain or coffee-flavoured marbled cake or sponge cake, cut into bite-sized pieces

whole seedless grapes

stoned and sliced firm peaches or nectarines

Arrange the dippers decoratively on a serving platter or individual serving plates and set aside.

Put the chocolate in the top of a double boiler or in a heatproof bowl set over a saucepan of barely simmering water, ensuring that the bowl does not touch the water. Add the cream and coffee granules and heat, stirring, until melted and smooth. Remove from the heat and stir in the liqueur, then carefully pour the mixture into a warmed fondue pot.

Using protective gloves, transfer the fondue pot to a lit tabletop burner. To serve, allow your guests to spear the dippers onto fondue forks and dip them into the fondue.

Sponge Cake with Custard

serves 4

125 g/4½ oz butter, plus extra for greasing

4 tbsp golden syrup

85 g/3 oz caster sugar

2 eggs, lightly beaten

125 g/4½ oz self-raising flour

1 tsp baking powder

about 2 tbsp warm water

custard, to serve

Grease a 1.5-litre/2¾-pint pudding basin with a little of the butter. Spoon the syrup into the prepared basin.

Beat the remaining butter with the sugar in a bowl until pale and fluffy. Gradually add the eggs, beating well after each addition.

Sift the flour and baking powder together, then gently fold into the butter mixture using a large metal spoon. Add enough water to give a soft, dropping consistency. Spoon the mixture into the basin and level the surface.

Cover with microwave-safe film, leaving a small space to let the air escape. Cook in a microwave oven on high for 4 minutes, then remove and leave the pudding to stand for 5 minutes while it continues to cook.

Turn the pudding out onto a serving plate. Serve with custard.

Pineapple Dessert

serves 6

1 pineapple

4 tbsp sultanas

2 tbsp raisins

4 tbsp maple syrup

4 tbsp white rum,
such as Bacardi

1 egg yolk

1 tbsp cornflour

½ tsp vanilla extract

¼ tsp ground ginger

2 egg whites

2 tbsp muscovado sugar

Preheat the oven to 240°C/475°F/Gas Mark 9. Cut off the leafy top and the base of the pineapple and discard. Stand the pineapple upright and slice off the skin. Remove any remaining 'eyes' with the tip of a small, sharp knife. Cut the pineapple in half lengthways and cut out the hard, woody core, then slice the flesh.

Arrange the pineapple slices in a large, ovenproof dish and sprinkle over the sultanas and raisins. Drizzle with half the maple syrup and half the rum. Bake in the preheated oven for 5 minutes.

Meanwhile, mix the remaining maple syrup and rum, egg yolk, cornflour, vanilla extract and ginger together in a bowl. Whisk the egg whites in a separate, spotlessly clean, grease-free bowl until soft peaks form. Stir 2 tablespoons of the egg whites into the egg yolk mixture, then fold the remaining egg yolk mixture into the egg whites.

Spread the topping over the hot pineapple, sift the sugar over the top and bake in the oven for a further 5 minutes, or until golden brown. Serve immediately.

Sweet & Spicy Wraps

makes 4

1 large mango, peeled and cut into large pieces

1 small pineapple, peeled cored and cut into large chunks

4 tbsp Greek yogurt

3 tbsp honey

4 x 25-cm/10-inch plain wraps

1 tbsp butter, melted

1 tsp allspice

Preheat the grill to high.

Mix together the mango, pineapple, yogurt and honey.

Brush the wraps with butter, sprinkle with allspice and place under the grill for 1 minute. This will add some colour and soften the wraps.

Divide the fruit mixture between the wraps, placing a portion down the middle of each. Fold in the ends, roll up and serve.

Lemon Posset

serves 4

grated rind and juice of
1 large lemon

4 tbsp dry white wine

55 g/2 oz caster sugar

300 ml/10 fl oz
double cream

2 egg whites

lemon slices, to decorate

langues de chat biscuits,
to serve

Mix the lemon rind and juice, wine and sugar together in a bowl. Stir until the sugar has dissolved. Add the cream and beat with a hand-held electric whisk until soft peaks form.

Whisk the egg whites in a separate, spotlessly clean, grease-free bowl until stiff, then gently fold into the cream mixture.

Spoon the mixture into tall glasses, cover and leave to chill in the refrigerator until required. Serve decorated with lemon slices and accompanied by langues de chat biscuits.

Fruit Skewers

makes 4

a selection of fruit, such as apricots, peaches, figs, strawberries, mangoes, pineapple, bananas, dates and pawpaw, prepared and cut into chunks

maple syrup

50 g/1¾ oz plain chocolate (minimum 70% cocoa solids), broken into chunks

Soak 4 bamboo skewers in water for at least 20 minutes.

Preheat the grill to high and line the grill pan with foil. Thread alternate pieces of fruit onto each skewer. Brush the fruit with a little maple syrup.

Put the chocolate in a heatproof bowl, set the bowl over a saucepan of barely simmering water, ensuring that the bowl does not touch the water, and heat until it is melted.

Meanwhile, cook the skewers under the preheated grill for 3 minutes, or until caramelized. Serve drizzled with a little of the melted chocolate.

Grilled Honeyed Figs with Sabayon

serves 4

8 ripe fresh figs, halved

4 tbsp clear honey

leaves from 2 fresh rosemary sprigs, finely chopped (optional)

3 eggs

Preheat the grill to high. Arrange the figs, cut-side up, on the grill rack. Brush with half the honey and scatter over the rosemary, if using.

Cook under the preheated grill for 5–6 minutes, or until just beginning to caramelize.

Meanwhile, to make the sabayon, lightly whisk the eggs with the remaining honey in a large, heatproof bowl, then set over a saucepan of simmering water. Using a hand-held electric whisk, beat the eggs and honey together for 10 minutes, or until pale and thick.

Put four fig halves on each of four serving plates, add a generous spoonful of the sabayon and serve immediately.

Griddled Bananas

serves 4

55 g/2 oz creamed coconut, chopped

150 ml/5 fl oz double cream

4 bananas

juice and finely grated rind of 1 lime, plus 1 lime, cut into wedges

1 tbsp vegetable or groundnut oil

50 g/1¾ oz desiccated coconut

Put the creamed coconut and cream in a small saucepan and heat over a low heat until the coconut has dissolved. Remove from the heat and leave to cool for 10 minutes, then whisk until thick but floppy.

Preheat a griddle pan over a high heat. Peel the bananas and toss in the lime juice and rind. Brush the preheated griddle pan with the oil, add the bananas and cook, turning once, for 2–3 minutes until soft and brown. Add the lime wedges halfway through the cooking time.

Meanwhile, preheat the grill to medium. Toast the desiccated coconut on a piece of foil under the preheated grill until lightly browned. Serve the bananas with the lime wedges and coconut cream, sprinkled with the coconut.

Nectarine Crunch

serves 3

4 nectarines

175 g/6 oz raisin and nut crunchy oat cereal

300 ml/10 fl oz low-fat natural yogurt

2 tbsp peach jam

2 tbsp peach nectar

Using a sharp knife, cut the nectarines in half, then remove and discard the stones. Chop the flesh into bite-sized pieces. Reserve a few pieces for decoration and put a few of the remaining pieces in the bottom of each of 3 sundae glasses. Put a layer of oat cereal in each glass, then drizzle over a little of the yogurt.

Put the jam and peach nectar in a large jug and stir together to mix. Add a few more nectarine pieces to the glasses and drizzle over a little of the jam mixture. Continue building up the layers in this way, finishing with a layer of yogurt and a sprinkling of oat cereal. Decorate with the reserved nectarine pieces and serve.

Grilled Cinnamon Oranges

serves 6

4 large oranges

1 tsp ground cinnamon

1 tbsp demerara sugar

Preheat the grill to high. Cut the oranges in half and discard any pips. Using a sharp knife or a curved grapefruit knife, carefully cut the flesh away from the skin by cutting around the edge of the fruit. Cut across the segments to loosen the flesh into bite-sized pieces that will then spoon out easily.

Arrange the orange halves, cut-side up, in a shallow, flameproof dish. Mix the cinnamon with the sugar in a small bowl and sprinkle evenly over the orange halves.

Cook under the preheated grill for 3–5 minutes, or until the sugar has caramelized and is golden and bubbling. Serve immediately.